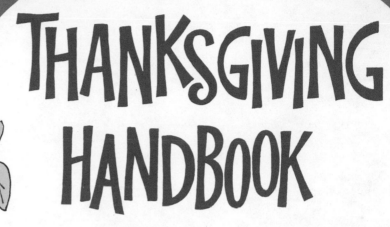

THANKSGIVING HANDBOOK

by Dotti Hannum
Betty Foster
Beth Holzbauer
Sandi Veranos
Annetta Dellinger
Dorothy Farrow
Paulette Lutz Glenn
Helen Bauman
Jane Belk Moncure
and others

illustrated by Gwen Connelly

THE CHILD'S WORLD

ELGIN, ILLINOIS 60120

EDITOR: Sandra Ziegler
CONTRIBUTING EDITOR: Diane Dow Suire

Distributed by Childrens Press, 1224 West Van Buren Street,
Chicago, Illinois 60607.

Library of Congress Cataloging in Publication Data

Main entry under title:

Thanksgiving handbook.

1. Thanksgiving Day.   2. Thanksgiving decorations.
I. Hannum, Dotti.   II. Connelly, Gwen.
GT4975.T47   1985   394.2'683   84-15536
ISBN 0-89565-269-2

1 2 3 4 5 6 7 8 9 10 11 12 R 90 89 88 87 86 85

THANKSGIVING HANDBOOK

USING THIS HANDBOOK

(For teachers of students in grades K-3)

Thanksgiving is coming. What will you do during November to make school an interesting place to be? What will you emphasize?

INDIANS? You'll want to pay special attention to the learning center ideas. But you'll find exciting ideas to adapt in every section.

PILGRIMS? The plans for the Thanksgiving Festival should stir your creative juices and give you enough ideas to fill the whole month.

HARVESTS AND FESTIVALS? Look for special ideas in the sections on Holiday History and Traditions and Symbols.

ALL OF THE ABOVE? Use the Table of Contents to find crafts, cooking ideas, poems, songs, games, and more. Students will agree. Learning is fun.

HAPPY THANKSGIVING.

CONTENTS

HOLIDAY HISTORY

by Betty Foster

If I asked you to tell me why we have Thanksgiving, would you tell me about the Pilgrims? Most Americans would.

It's true. The Pilgrims did celebrate the first American Thanksgiving in Plymouth in December, 1621.

The Pilgrims had many reasons to be thankful. They had survived their first hard winter. They had learned to hunt in the forests and fish in the sea. They could grow corn and other food in their fields. They had made Indian friends. The Pilgrims were feeling good about life in America.

But the Pilgrims were not the first people to find reasons to be thankful and decide to celebrate.

Long ago the Greeks and Romans celebrated at harvest time after their work was done and their food was safely stored away. So did people in Egypt, China, Japan, India, and Africa. They even gave some of their best foods to their gods as part of their celebrations.

In England, even before the Pilgrims came to America, people celebrated a special day, called *Harvest Home*, at wheat-harvest time. To start that celebration, harvesters lifted the person who had cut the last sheaf of wheat, along with his wife or girl friend, to the top of a flower-covered cart loaded with the last of the wheat. They sang and danced alongside the cart as it made its way to a feast.

In America, the second Thanksgiving was celebrated in 1623. That year the Pilgrims celebrated because a ship came from England, bringing supplies which they badly needed. In the years after that, people in America often celebrated harvest festivals. But they did not celebrate in every town, and no one celebrated every year.

In 1789 President George Washington decided that people all over the country should celebrate a nationwide Thanksgiving in the United States. But celebrations were still infrequent. Americans celebrated Thanksgiving Day some years and some years they didn't.

For twenty years Mrs. Sara Hale tried to have Thanksgiving made a national holiday, the way the Fourth of July was. When Abraham Lincoln became President, he made it a holiday.

Today Thanksgiving Day is the fourth Thursday of November. Most Americans get together to eat a turkey dinner, share the good times, and give thanks. Some people celebrate by watching big parades, such as Macy's Parade in New York. They enjoy the bands, floats, and balloons. Other people spend the day watching football games. How do you celebrate on Thanksgiving Day?

BEFORE THE RUSH

(Preparation Ideas for November Units)

INDIANS NEAR AND FAR

Do you live in a part of the country where you have Indians close by? Find out about the Indians near you. Contrast them with Indians from other tribes. How are they alike? How are they different? See if you can arrange for a tribal member to visit your class and talk with the children.

INDIAN DISPLAYS

Begin to collect samples of Indian arts, crafts, and arrowheads. Plan how you will display the collection. It is likely that your pupils will have items to show and share, and you will want to put them on exhibit too.

Explain to your class about the special Indian displays ahead of time. Tell the children you will display what they bring, such as Indian dolls, moccasins, dresses, headdresses, feathers, canoes, beads, etc. You'll be surprised at what appears for this special table!

LIVING MUSEUM

Is there a museum or tourist attraction in your area where your students may see live demonstrations of how the pioneers made brooms and pots, how they

gathered wood, made thread, wove cloth, and made clothes? Plan a field trip, or find out if some of the exhibitors will come to you.

A THANKSGIVING FESTIVAL

Today at Plymouth, Massachusetts, there are many tourist attractions to help people understand more about the Pilgrims. A replica of their ship, called *Mayflower II,* is anchored in the harbor near Plymouth Rock. It was a gift built by the British. In 1957, they sailed it

to Plymouth in fifty-three days. Now people can go aboard to see what the *Mayflower* was like. Nearby is a statue of the Pilgrims' Indian friend, Massasoit. Two and one-half miles away is "Plimoth Plantation," a living example of a Pilgrim village in 1627. People dressed as Pilgrims "live" in the tiny houses. They go about many of the necessary tasks for their 17th century world. Gardens, corn fields, and live sheep and chickens add to the reality when you explore this fascinating place. Teachers may request an information portfolio about the village by sending requests to: Plimoth Plantation, The 1627 Pilgrim Village, Plymouth, Massachusetts 02360.

Not everyone can visit Plymouth and learn about the Pilgrims. Because of that, you may want to recreate the first Thanksgiving celebration right in your classroom. The ideas on pages 67-72 will help you think of ways to do that. Some ideas may be harder to work out

than others. You will want to choose and adapt ideas to meet your needs. Even if you don't have an elaborate Thanksgiving festival, you may still want to use some of the suggestions in this section.

If you decide to have a dinner as part of your festival, you will be able to choose from menu ideas and recipes (see pages 48-50 and 71). If you do not plan a dinner, you may still want to invite a group in to see your displays and enjoy a program put on by the "Pilgrims" and "Indians" in costumes.

Pages 16-24 feature ideas for Thanksgiving room decorations. Incorporate some of the ideas into your plans, or choose from these suggestions.

FOOD ARRANGEMENTS: If you can gather pumpkins, squash, apples, potatoes, Indian corn, leaves, wheat, dried flowers, nuts, and so forth, let the children make groupings of these items for the centers of the tables. Also use cornucopias if you have them. You will want to cover the tables with paper cloths before you do the arrangements.

DRIED FLOWERS: Before frost kills the flowers, ask your students to gather bouquets. Dry the flowers. Make flower arrangements for your festival tables from the flowers which you have dried. For vases, use hollowed-out pumpkins, or have the pupils make vases decorated with Indian symbols. It takes a week or two to dry flowers. It is a good idea to consult a book on how to do it.

KERNEL BAGS: Have a few children prepare the bags as described here for use at the Thanksgiving festival (see pages 67-72).

Place five kernels of candy corn and a copy of the Legend of the Five Kernels (see below) in a small plastic bag. Tie closed with orange yarn or ribbon. Make one bag for each person at the Thanksgiving festival.

THE LEGEND OF THE FIVE KERNELS

The first winter the Pilgrims spent in their new home was very cold. Food was in short supply. Some days they had only enough food for each person to have five kernels of corn for the day. But spring came. They planted food. It grew. And all the Pilgrims did not die. From then on, when a time of Thanksgiving came around, the Pilgrims put five kernels of corn on each plate and used them to remind themselves of their blessings. Let us also remember: (hold up each kernel one at a time as you read about it).

The first kernel reminds us of the autumn beauty around us.

The second kernel reminds us of our love for each other.

The third kernel reminds us of God's love and care for us.

The fourth kernel reminds us of our friends—especially our Indian brothers.

The fifth kernel reminds us we are free people.

AROUND
THE ROOM

ROOM DECORATIONS

Nothing helps set the mood for a holiday as much as colorful decorations. And they can serve as reminders of important people, places, or things you want to remember about a holiday. Choose from ideas here to create a Thanksgiving atmosphere in your classroom.

PAPER PLATE TURKEY

You will need paper plates, crayons or markers, red chenille wire, construction paper, and glue.

Explain to the children: use the brown construction paper to cut out a body for your turkey (see illustration for how). Use the orange construction paper to make a turkey's head. Glue them onto a paper plate. (Demonstrate each step.)

Draw eyes on the turkey's head. Either draw a red wattle on the turkey's face or glue on a snipet of red chenille wire for the wattle.

Draw two legs and feet for the turkey. Then color the top ⅔ of the plate to look like the turkey's feathers. Color the bottom ⅓ to look like grass.

by Beth Holzbauer

COOKIE TURKEY

Do this activity prior to your Thanksgiving party. Then you can use the *"cookie turkeys"* for table decorations.

Provide one large round cookie, one Nutter-Butter sandwich cookie, three sugar wafers (assorted flavors), two chocolate chips, a snip from a red licorice string, sandwich bag, and white frosting for each child.

Have the children use frosting to stick the sandwich cookie onto the round cookie as the turkey's head and also to stick the other pieces together. Stick on chocolate chip eyes, licorice wattle and three different-colored sugar wafers for feathers. Store cookie in bag.

by Beth Holzbauer

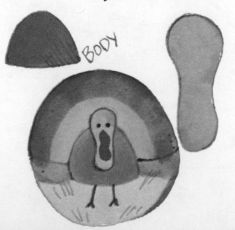

16

PILGRIM PEOPLE MOBILES

To make the mobiles you will need construction paper, white ribbon, gold paper, scissors, glue, and yarn.

For a PILGRIM BOY make a hat from black construction paper (cut as illustrated). Cut all the pieces double so that you can glue them back to back. Decorate the hat with a piece of ribbon and a gold paper buckle. Cut a collar as illustration shows.

Cut a paper rectangle. Glue on eyes, nose, hair, and mouth from appropriate colors of construction paper.

Turn hat, face, and collar over. Tape face behind the hat and collar.

Add hanger of yarn at top. Cover the hat and collar with matching pieces and glue in place.

Hang the mobile where it will move in the air currents.

For a PILGRIM GIRL cut a cap and collar. Glue hair—made of fringed yellow or brown construction paper—in the cap at the top of the head. Glue rectangle for face behind hat and collar. Also add yarn for hanging mobile. Then glue matching pieces together to cover the tape.

Make facial features.

Glue eyes, nose, and mouth to facial rectangle to complete mobile. Hang it where the air currents will move it about.

INDIAN TEPEE

When Indians built a tepee, they alway left an opening at the top. That was so the smoke, which would rise from the fire inside, could go out through the top.

Have the children make a tepee for the room. Allow one or two children at a time in the tepee. It's a great place for reading quietly!

To make a tepee you will need three 6' poles, heavy twine or wire, clay, rolls of brown paper, masking or electrical tape, bright colors of tempera or poster paint, brushes, and scissors.

Let the children help as you wire or tie the three poles together loosely at the top with heavy twine or cord. Tie the poles together at about 1½ feet from top. (Tree branches make great poles. Or buy bamboo poles at a home center or fishing tackle store.)

Use clay to anchor the poles to the floor.

With masking or electrical tape, attach the brown roll paper to the frame.

Have the children paint Indian designs on the brown paper. Use

brightly-colored tempera or poster paint to do this.

Let the paint dry. Then cut a door in the brown covering. Fold the door back to make the entrance.

by Dotti Hannum

TOTEM POLE

For this project you will need three to five cardboard boxes, brown butcher or craft paper approximately the same size as the boxes, two large sheets of poster board or cardboard, tempera and brushes, glue, and masking tape.

Cover the boxes with brown paper. Divide the children into groups. Let each group paint a face on each side of a box. Let the boxes dry.

Glue the boxes together, one on top of the other.

Cut wings out of two large pieces of cardboard. Have some children paint the wings.

Use masking tape to attach the wings to the totem pole.

by Dotti Hannum

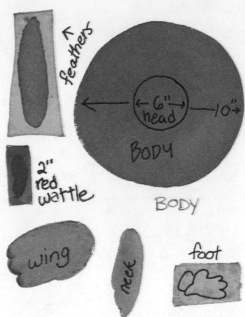

DOOR AND WINDOW
TURKEYS

To make large turkeys, nearly twenty inches tall, you will need brown, tan, yellow, white, black, and red construction paper in 12-by-18-inch sheets; scissors; and glue.

Older pupils will be able to cut their own turkeys after you show them how. You may want to prepare some of the pieces for younger students to use. Make a sample to show the children what they will be making.

Here's how you do it. From two sheets of brown paper cut identical 10-inch circles. Cut two tan wings, two necks, and two 6-inch round heads (see sketches for how to do this freehand). Also cut two red

wattles and two pairs of yellow feet.

Cut tail feathers from brown, tan, and yellow paper. To glue the turkeys together, first glue feathers to the back of one of the 10-inch circles. Then glue the two circles together.

Glue a wing to each side of the bird.

Match the neck pieces. Glue them to each side of the turkey so they match. Add head and wattle pieces back to back.

Add feet. Glue them on each side of the bird so they line up.

Put eyes on each side of the head. Your turkey is now ready to hang in a window, or on a door or bulletin board.

NOVEMBER BULLETIN BOARDS

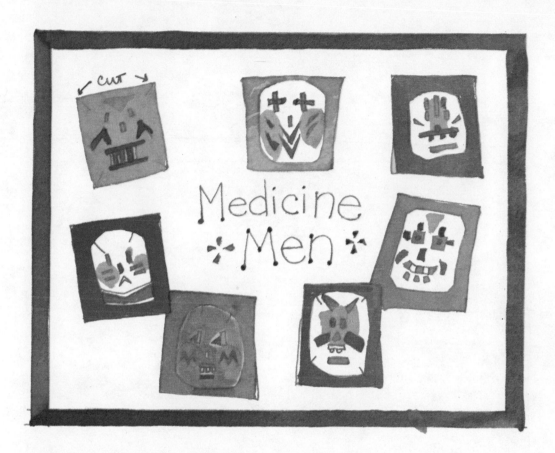

MEDICINE MEN MASKS

Medicine Men Masks make an attractive bulletin board display. Mount each one on a black background. Caption the board "Medicine Men."

To make masks, you will need 12-by-18-inch sheets of brightly colored construction paper, foil, other decorative materials, and glue or paste.

To make a mask, slit all four corners of a sheet of construction paper as in illustration.

Overlap the corners and staple each corner to make a three-dimensional piece. Cut eye opening if desired.

Decorate with features made from scraps, foil, etc. Use bright colors. Be creative! Masks may have weird designs.

by Dotti Hannum

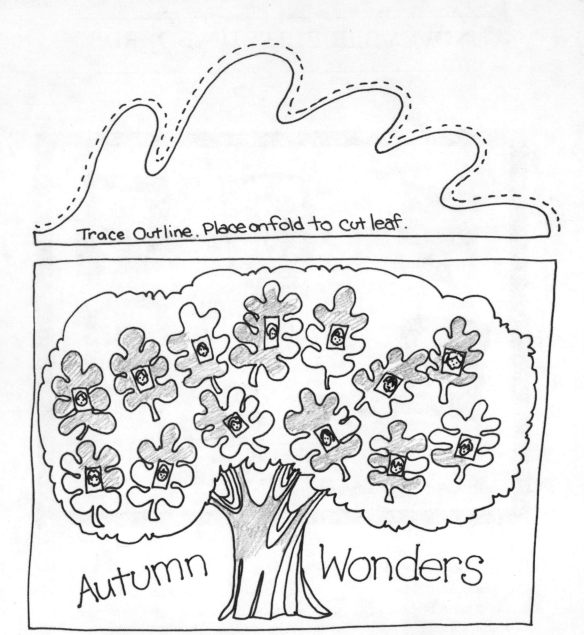

Trace Outline. Place on fold to cut leaf.

AUTUMN WONDERS

Cut out leaves of various colors from construction paper. Also make a large black or brown tree trunk. Cut a small hole in the center of each leaf. Place each child's picture on the back of a leaf and let his smiling face show through. Display the leaves on the bulletin board. Use a gold treetop as the background. You might caption the board "Autumn Wonders."

by Annetta Dellinger

WHO IS THANKFUL?

SEED ACTIVITY: Decorate the top of a small jar and bring it to class. Tell the children this will be their "thankful" jar. Pass out two seeds to each child. Tell the children to think of two things they are thankful for. As you call on each child, he is to come up, tell what he is thankful for, and put his seeds in the "thankful" jar. When everyone is finished, the jar should be full. Keep the jar on display in your room to remind the children of their thankfulness. Refer to the jar as the "thankful" jar. Following this activity, have the children make the seed pictures for the bulletin board.

SEED PICTURES: Provide a variety of seeds, yarn or cording, alphabet macaroni, cottage cheese container lids, felt, glue, and tissue paper.

Before class, cut a felt circle—the size of the inner circle in the cottage cheese lid—for each child. Let him glue the felt to the lid.

Each person should draw an outline on his felt picture of a food item he is thankful for—corn, apple, beans, etc. Provide simple patterns if you feel it is necessary. Then the child should glue yarn around the outline.

Next let the child fill in the outline with seeds to add color and dimension. Then he may add tissue-paper leaves.

At the top of the picture, the child may glue on letters to spell GIVE THANKS.

Ask an assistant to label each picture. Each child may put his name on his picture. Hang the pictures and labels, with the caption, "I am thankful for. . .," on the bulletin board.

by Beth Holzbauer

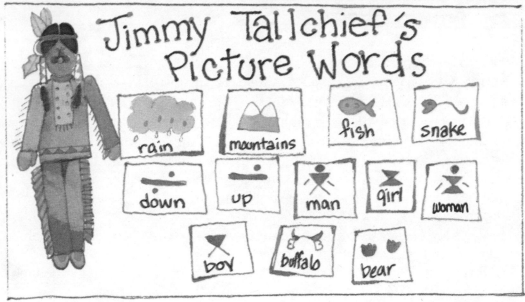

JIMMY TALLCHIEF'S PICTURE WORDS

In advance, prepare some Indian picture word cards with captions. You may use assorted colors of construction paper for this. Also cut out and decorate a tall Indian similiar to the one illustrated. Then prepare the caption.

Pin the display to your bulletin board. If space permits, invite the students to think of other picture words and make the pictures. Add their pictures to the display. Older students may make up stories and write them in Indian picture writing.

LEARNING
CENTERS

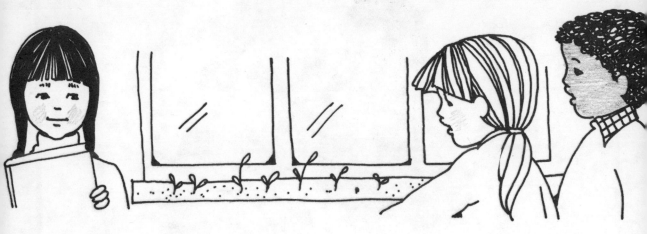

WATCHING THINGS GROW

Since you will be thinking a lot about what we eat during November, encourage the children to plant and grow some foods.

SANDWICH SPROUTS

If you try this learning center idea, you'll need to provide quart-sized wide-mouth jars with lids, cheesecloth or a fine strainer, radish or alfalfa seeds, and a water source.

You'll want to explain this procedure to the class as a whole and also post the directions in the learning center so students can work independently.

For each jar you will need about two tablespoons of seeds.

STEP ONE: Place the seeds into the jar.

STEP TWO: Cover seeds with water and allow them to soak overnight.

STEP THREE: In the morning, cover the jar with cheesecloth or use a strainer (so the seeds don't go down the drain), then pour off the water.

STEP FOUR: Rinse the seeds again and drain.

STEP FIVE: Shake the seeds around inside the jar. Cover the jar with a cloth, and let it rest on its side in a warm place.

Each morning and each afternoon the students should rinse and drain the seeds. As they begin to sprout, some of the hulls will wash away. Do this step every day for three to five days until the sprouts are big enough to eat.

When the children have grown their sprouts, let them make sandwiches, using pita bread. Stuff some of the home-grown sprouts into the sandwiches.

POTATO BASKETS

Set up a learning center in your room with large potatoes, potting soil, mustard seeds, chenille wire, sharp knives, spoons, plastic can lids, ribbon bows, and suitable work space for planting.

Have clear instructions posted in the center, and have an aide help students. Each student needs a plastic lid and a large potato. The aide should help the student cut off the top and bottom of the potato.

The child should place one cut end of his potato on the lid. Then he should use a spoon to hollow out some of the potato.

Each child may fill his potato with soil and plant the mustard seeds.

The student should bend a long chenille wire like a basket handle and insert each end into his potato.

He should add a ribbon bow. He may want to contrast the ribbon colors to the chenille wire or use a fall color.

Water the seeds, and let the children watch the plants sprout and grow. Each pupil should keep track of his plant's progress.

For each student who visits this learning center, you might want to provide a calendar sheet that has a day space large enough for the child to describe the plant growth.

Let younger students watch for signs of growth and draw what they see in the appropriate day spaces on their calendar sheets.

Talk about how the plants vary in size and growing time. See if students have ideas about why there are differences.

PERKY TURKEY'S RHYME-TIME FUN

Follow the directions on page 20 for making a large turkey. Instead of using construction paper, use poster board so that you can make a 20-inch body for a much larger bird. Put your turkey where all the children may see it. Ask children to suggest words that make them think of Thanksgiving. Write the words on the turkey.

Explain to the children that you will hang the turkey in the Rhyme-Time Area. When they have some extra time, students may visit the area. They may see how many of the words on the list they can rhyme with other words. Let an aide assist younger students. Older students may want to take some of their rhymed couplets and write a poem. Encourage them to do so. Ask the students to give you their papers when they are finished in the area. When all the children have visited the center, read some of the sheets, and see how many different words the children thought of to rhyme with the words on the list. Share some of the poems.

TALKING TOGETHER IN SIGNS

Beforehand, explain that most of us talk to each other with words. But what would we do to tell each other things if one of us could not hear? Yes, we might write notes or draw pictures. We might also talk in signs. The Indians often used signs to talk with each other. (Deaf people use signs in talking with each other. Perhaps you can invite someone to talk to the children about this.) Make some posters using Indian signs, and put them in a spot for a learning center. (See signs below for help in doing this.)

Then let the children visit the center two at a time. The two can practice telling each other things using signs. They can also think up and make other signs. You may want to provide Indian costumes for students to wear so they can pretend to be Indians signing to each other. (This will be especially helpful for shy students.)

by Dotti Hannum

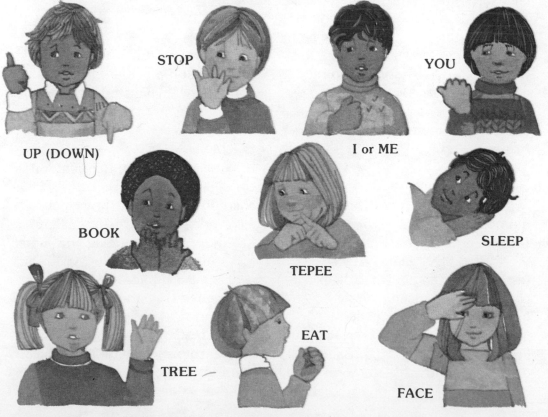

STOP

YOU

UP (DOWN)

I or ME

BOOK

TEPEE

SLEEP

TREE

EAT

FACE

29

INDIAN THREE SISTERS

People in New England used to call the three crops the Indians depended on most, "the Indian Three Sisters." The crops were corn, beans, and squash. In this center let pupils do some of the suggested activities to develop an appreciation of the three important foods the Indians shared with the Pilgrims.

CORN

If you have a copy of the sequence chart, *The Story of Corn* (available from The Child's World, P.O. Box 989, Elgin, IL 60121), put it up in the center to help the children understand how corn grows.

Bring some ears of corn for the center. Let the children husk them. Provide some dried corn and some smooth rocks. Let the students crush corn and grind it into meal.

BEANS

Bring some dried beans. Let the students sort and soak them. Then cook them. Have students observe the changes in the beans.

SQUASH

Put a selection of different kinds of squash in the center. Have children tell an aide how they are alike and how they are different. Let them cook some of the kinds of squash—especially spaghetti squash (see page 48). Let the children try it with some spaghetti sauce on it.

As a math activity let the children count squash seeds and divide them into sets.

WHAT MADE THE MAYFLOWER GO?

Before students visit this learning center, show them a picture of a modern ship. Talk about what makes the ship move. Then show students a picture of the Mayflower. Ask what made it move.

At the learning center, the students can work independently making soap boats—if the procedure is first demonstrated, and instructions are posted.

You'll need to trace the pattern below onto cardboard. Students can use the cardboard pattern to trace and make a sail for their own soap boats. You'll also need to provide paper (for the sails), scissors, toothpicks, tape, bars of soap for each student, table coverings, a washtub of water, and a fan.

Explain, then post directions:

STEP ONE: Trace the sail pattern on white paper.

STEP TWO: Cut out the sail.

STEP THREE: Tape the sail to the toothpick.

STEP FOUR: Push the toothpick into the soap.

STEP FIVE: Put your boat in the washtub of water. Does it sail?

STEP SIX: Turn on the fan. What happens?

STEP SEVEN: Turn off the fan. Take your boat out of the water. Put it on the newspaper. Print your name next to your boat.

pattern for sail

Yellow Blossom

Candy Lover

Spotted Pony

Sun Bright

Moon Boots

Green Pea

Black Bird

Brown Puppy

Blue Balloon

Star Bright

Violet

Red Bike

Mountain Climber

Burger Kid

White Cloud

Little Raindrops

Kite Flyer

Strawberry Ice Cream

Star Shower

Good Jumper

Yellow Bird

Bell Ringer

Blue Bird

Yellow House

Tent Camper

Little Rainbow

Green Fish

Green Turtle

Moonlight

Green Grass

Juice

Top Banana

Apple Eater

WHICH PICTURE ARE YOU?

Talk with the children about how Indian names were different from their names. Indian children had names that told something about them. Some examples: Little Pale Moon, Rising Moon, Running Bear, Bird Woman, Sitting Bull, Little Cloud, Three Stars. (Of course, their names were said in Indian words and didn't sound like the English names do.)

Each of the children has something special about himself that could be used to create an Indian picture name that would identify the child. Set up a learning center where students can go and work with an aide to think up picture names that suit them. The aide will need to work with one or two children at a time until all the children have picture names that they can draw.

Let the children make autograph books and collect the picture names of other classmates. Then let the children tell why they chose the names they did.

GAMES
AND RHYTHMIC
ACTIVITIES

THANKS BINGO

Older students will enjoy playing this game. Make and duplicate cards (see illustration) with 9, 12, or 16 squares. Also provide corn kernels to use as markers.

Have the children help you list ten to twenty Thanksgiving words. List the words on the board. Have each child print words at *random* in each square on his card. Words should *not* be in the order listed. Also print each word on a small slip of paper. Put in a box.

Choose a child who will draw and call out one word at a time from the box containing all the words. At their seats, the children will cover the squares containing each word as it is called. The first one to cover all the words in a row (across, down, or diagonally) gets to call words next.

by Betty Foster

PUMPKIN TOSS UP

Materials: 12-by-18-inch sheets of orange construction paper, scissors, crayons or felt-tip pens, paste or glue, paper or styrofoam cups.

Explain to the children as follows: first fold a sheet of orange construction paper in half and glue it together. Draw and cut out ten pumpkins. (Pumpkins must not be larger than the diameter of the cups. The pattern here could be used as a size guide.)

Number one side of each pumpkin. Number the pumpkins in order 1-10.

Place all ten pumpkins inside a cup, and you are ready to play the game. How you play depends upon your rules and how good you are at adding.

SUGGESTED WAYS TO PLAY

1. Toss the pumpkins into the air. Catch as many as you can in the cup. Count them. Score one point for each one you catch.

2. Toss the pumpkins into the air. Let them fall on the floor. Add up the numbers you can read.

3. Toss the pumpkins into the air. Let them fall. Get one point for each number you see and can read.

PASS THE "THANKERCHIEF"

Have the children stand in a circle. Pass the "thankerchief" (a handkerchief) around the circle as the children say:

Thankerchief, thankerchief,
around you go—
Where you'll stop, we don't
know.
But when you do, someone must
say,
What we are thankful for this
day.

When the verse ends, the person holding the "thankerchief" must tell one thing he is thankful for. That person then steps out of the circle and the verse begins again. The game continues until there is only one child left standing. The class then repeats the verse, giving the last person a chance to tell what he is thankful for. Encourage the children to think of different things, but repeats should be acceptable.

by Beth Holzbauer

THE TURKEY HUNT

On five strips of paper write "turkey". On other strips (one for each child minus eight) write names of other birds and animals that make noises, such as cow, dog, cat.

Choose three children to be Pilgrims. Explain that the rest of the children will be animals or birds.

To play, have all the children, except the three Pilgrims, draw names. Nobody should tell what he is.

The birds and animals should spread out around the room. Let the first Pilgrim go hunting. He should walk up to one of the students and say, "Bang, bang!" The student should answer with his animal sound (a cow would answer "MOO!"). If the student is a turkey, he should answer, "Gobble, gobble." Then he must stay with the Pilgrim for the Thanksgiving feast. If the student is not a turkey, he remains in his place. The other Pilgrims should watch and not "shoot" the wrong animals again.

Give each Pilgrim three chances to find the turkeys. When all the Pilgrims have gone hunting, count up the turkeys they have found. The scoring will go as follows:

5 turkeys: Super feast!
4 turkeys: No second helpings!
3 turkeys: Turkey sandwiches!
2 turkeys: TV dinners!
1 turkey: Turkey soup!
0 turkeys: No supper!

by Beth Holzbauer

SAYING THANK YOU

Use Thanksgiving to "brush up" on some good manners. First read and talk about a book on manners: *Saying Thank You*, by Colleen Reece, *Your Manners Are Showing*, by Eugene Baker, or *Please Pass the P's and Q's*, by Barbara Hazen. Emphasize the importance of being thankful and saying "thank you."

Give everyone (teacher too) empty paper cups and about twenty dried beans. During the day, if someone says "thank you for. . ." in response to something someone gives him or does for him, he should receive a bean from the person he says it to. The child then puts the bean in his cup. At the end of the day, put the "thank you" beans in one pile and count them. Award a prize to the class based on the number of beans everyone has collected. This will encourage the children to say "thank you" and do kind things for one another.

by Beth Holzbauer

LITTLE INDIAN BRAVE

I'm a little Indian. I wear feathers
   in my hat.
   *(Hold fingers to form feathers at
   back of head.)*
I have a bow and arrows.
   *(Crook left arm for bow; right
   hand holds arrows.)*
I wear them on my back.
   (Hang quiver on back.)
I sleep inside a tepee.
   *(Interlock fingertips to form
   tepee.)*
I fish in the brook for trout.
   (Cast fishing line.)
And when I'm feeling happy, I sing
   and dance about.
   (Do Indian dance in place.)
WHO-OO-OO-OO-OOO!
   *(Cover and uncover mouth with
   hand as you give a war cry.)*
                    by Dotti Hannum

MY TURKEY

My Thanksgiving turkey gobbler
   *(Hold up hand, palm toward
   audience, fingers together,
   thumb out.)*
Went prancing all about.
   *(Shake hand as you walk it
   about.)*
He shook his head.
   (Wiggle thumb.)
He fanned his tail,
   (Spread fingers apart.)
I thought he looked my way.
   *(Turn palm toward self, then
   back again.)*
But then he slipped out through the
   gate
   *(Dart "turkey" away under op-
   posite arm.)*
And missed Thanksgiving Day.
   (Fold arms in front of you.)

TEN LITTLE PILGRIMS

Ten little Pilgrims touched their toes.
  (Touch toes.)
Ten little Pilgrims picked a rose.
  (Stoop and pick rose.)
Ten little Pilgrims turned around.
  (Turn around.)
Ten little Pilgrims ran to town.
  (Run in place.)
Ten little Pilgrims skipped through a door.
  (Skip.)
Ten little Pilgrims sat on the floor.
  (Sit on floor.)
Ten little Pilgrims held out their hands.
  (Hold out hands as if giving away a flower.)
Ten little Pilgrims held roses grand.
  (Cup hands as if smelling a rose.)
Ten Pilgrims mothers clapped, you see.
  (Clap your hands.)
And each one asked, "Is that for me?"
  (Hold hands out, then point to self.)
Ten little Pilgrims nodded with delight.
  (Stand up; nod head in agreement.)
Ten little Pilgrims got hugged "just right."
  (Make hugging motion.)

by Sandra Ziegler

THINGS TO MAKE AND DO

INDIAN ACTIVITIES

INDIAN DANCING

Provide sticks, drums, and rattles. Some students may play the dance rhythm with the instruments as others dance. Those playing instruments should give a heavy beat on the capped words, lighter beats on other words.

"Walk" means to give a long, rhythmic tap.

"Run" means to give a short tap— two short taps equal one long tap.

The dancers should move slowly or quickly according to the beats. They may leap or bow slightly on accented beats.

After students learn the dance, they may enjoy wearing costumes as they perform for others.

W-A-L-K, w-a-l-k, W-A-L-K,
w-a-l-k,
RUN, run, run, run, RUN, run,
run, run.
(Keep repeating rhythm.)

by Dotti Hannum

INDIAN PAINTING

Indians used beets, wild berries, and other fruits and vegetables to make dyes to paint animal skins and ornaments. Sometimes when they got ready for a dance or pow-wow, they mixed the brightly colored dyes with animal fat so the colors would stick to their faces and bodies.

To do some Indian painting you will need canned beet slices, canned blueberries, and one piece of muslin for each child.

Have each child "stamp" some of the beet slices and blueberries on his square of muslin to create a picture. Let the painting dry overnight. Then press it.

To hang the paintings, the children may use push pins.

by Dotti Hannum

Another way to do Indian painting is to clean and boil the following in separate pans: beets, spinach, cranberries, yellow onions. Let each student use the colored, boiled water to paint an Indian shirt.

Make each shirt from an old pillow case. Cut a slit in the top big enough for the child's head. Cut arm holes on each side. Fringe the bottom edge.

by Annetta Dellinger

MOON WATCHING

The Indians used the moon as a calendar. They knew that the full moon came in the night sky about every 28 days. Have the students make poster-sized calendar sheets for October and November. When the full moon comes in October, have the children begin to keep a record of the number of days from one full face of the moon to the next. Compare this with the number of days in our calendar month.

by Dotti Hannum

Fold paper in half.
Fold in half again.
Cut out Canoe shape.

CANOES

Indians made canoes from tree bark and dried animal skins. Their canoes were hollow and light. They could be paddled easily up or down a river.

To make Indian canoes you will need 8-by-12-inch sheets of brown construction paper, hole puncher and yarn, or stapler and staples, crayons, felt markers, or colored chalk.

Explain to the pupils: first cut matching canoe shapes from brown paper (see sketch).

Then decorate one side of each shape with Indian signs. Use crayons, markers, or colored chalk to do this.

Finally, either punch holes along the bottom edge of each piece and "sew" the two canoes together with yarn, or staple the pieces together around the bottom and sides.

Some children may want to make paper Indians with paddles and glue them inside their canoes.

by Dotti Hannum

INDIAN COSTUMES

Let pupils make and wear Indian costumes for Thanksgiving. You will also find suggestions for Indian pants and headdresses on page 79, which you may add to the costume ideas here.

INDIAN VESTS: You will need large paper bags, scissors, and markers, paints, or crayons.

Cut a slit up the front of each paper bag. Cut a neck opening in the top. Then cut armholes from the sides.

Let the children cut fringe around the bottoms of the bags with scissors.

They may use the markers, crayons, or paints to decorate the vests with Indian pictures.

WAMPUM NECKLACES: Indians did not have money. They traded objects or services for what they wanted. Some Indians used wampum—purple and white beads made from shells—as money. The Indians made necklaces and belts with wampum. To make wampum necklaces, you will need pieces of elbow macaroni, straws (white or colored), tempera, scissors, paint brushes, twine—18-inch lengths, and newspaper.

Let the students paint pieces of uncooked macaroni in various colors. Spread the macaroni out on newspaper and let it dry.

Pupils may also cut drinking straws into 1-inch pieces.

Each child may string macaroni and straws on an 18-inch length of twine to make a necklace. Tie the ends of the twine together and slip the necklace on and off over the head.

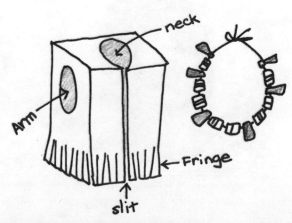

PILGRIM ACTIVITIES

FLOUR/SALT CLAY BEADS

If the Pilgrims had extra flour and salt, they sometimes used it to make clay for the children.

To make clay beads you will need four cups of flour, two cups of salt, some water, a mixing bowl, waxed paper, toothpicks, spool wire or thread and needles, paints and brushes, shellac or varnish.

First mix the flour and salt together. Add water, a little at a time, as you keep mixing the clay together with your hands. When the mixture is like dough, it's ready to use. (This mixture dries your hands, so you will want to have some hand lotion nearby to use when the activity is finished!)

Give each person some clay. The child can break his clay into bead-sized balls. Then he is ready to shape the beads—round, square, oblong, and so forth.

Tell the child to line up the beads the way he wants them when they are strung.

Let each child use a toothpick to carefully make a hole in each bead. He can put it on the wire (or whatever he is using to string the beads).

Allow the beads to air dry. Then let the children paint and shellac them.

by Dotti Hannum

HAND PRINT TURKEY

You will need crayons, construction paper, 9-by-12-inch manila paper, and glue.

Let the children pretend they are Pilgrim children who want to make some decorations. Explain that there are two ways to make a hand print turkey. One way is to lay your hand flat on a piece of drawing paper with all your fingers spread as far as they will go. Trace around your hand stopping at your wrist.

Do you see your turkey? (Show sample.) Color in his feathers, body, red wattle, eye, feet, even a top hat, if you wish. Then add background scenery.

STICK DOLL

Puppets or dolls were made of any materials the Pilgrims could find—cornhusks, sticks, corncobs, socks. Try easy-to-make dolls. Make them from tongue depressors or wooden spoons.

You will need glue, tongue depressors or wooden spoons, felt markers, material scraps, 9-inch squares of material (or paper tissues), cotton, yarn or corn silks for hair, and something to tie the necks.

Have each person draw facial features on the bowl of his wooden spoon or on one end of a tongue depressor. Use felt markers for this.

Let each child glue on cotton, yarn, or corn silks for hair. He may use his imagination and fabric scraps to make clothes.

Another way to make clothes is to fold a square of material diagonally. Place it around the doll, like a cape, and tie it. Or use a piece of yarn to fasten it. And wrap ends around the doll.

by Annetta Dellinger
and Betty Foster

Another way you could do it is to trace your hand with your fingers and thumb together, at an angle on your paper so your hand print becomes the turkey's tail. Then you may either draw the rest of the turkey or put it together with construction paper shapes—a circle for the body, a head shape, wattle, wing, and feet. (Show samples.)

by Dotti Hannum

GRAB AN IDEA

by Annetta Dellinger and Betty Foster

DRYING FOOD WE EAT

Indians dried food to keep it from spoiling. They dried meat and fish by hanging it in the sunshine. Sometimes they dried fruit the same way or over a fire.

We often dry food too. Show the children dried grapes/raisins, plums/prunes, apricots, apples, beef jerky, and fruit leather. Have everyone taste dried foods.

If you have facilities to do so, dry some fruit or make fruit leather. (For information about how to do this write to the California Tree Fruit Agreement, P.O. Box 255627, Sacramento, CA 95865. Ask for "Sunshine Preserving: Fresh Fruit Jerky." Be sure to send a self-addressed, stamped, business-sized envelope.)

THE TURKEY FARM

Visit a turkey farm. Ask permission to collect turkey feathers. Count them. Categorize them according to size, color, etc. Paint with them. Write with them.

LET'S COMPARE

For younger children, display pictures of four turkeys of different sizes. Learn the following verse:

"I'm the littlest (big, bigger) turkey but that's okay.
'Cause nobody wants the littlest (big, bigger) turkey on Thanksgiving Day!"

(Repeat for each size, then say:)

"I'm the biggest turkey so I'll run away.
'Cause everybody wants the biggest turkey on Thanksgiving Day!"

THANKSGIVING THEN AND NOW

Make two murals, each about 3-feet high and 5-feet long. Title the murals "The Pilgrims' First Thanksgiving" and "Thanksgiving Today."

As you talk with the children, make a list on the board of what to include in each mural to bring out differences and similarities between Thanksgiving then and now.

Divide the class into two groups. Each group will need to choose an artist to roughly sketch its mural.

Then each group will have to decide who will do the background, people, title, etc. The children may complete their assignments for the mural individually and then place their contributions together to make the murals.

SOMETHING'S COOKING

Your young cooks can have a great time preparing and learning about foods the Pilgrims enjoyed which are still nutritionally good for us today. Let your students experiment with one or more of the following recipes.

PUMPKIN PUDDING

1 cup canned pumpkin or squash
¼ t. salt
¼ t. cinnamon
¼ t. cloves

1 T. honey
1½ cups milk
1 package (3¾ oz.) instant
    vanilla pudding

Mix the pumpkin, salt, cinnamon, cloves, and honey together in a mixing bowl. Stir in the milk. Mix well. Add pudding and beat slowly about one minute until it thickens. Chill and serve. Makes three cups of pudding.

by Annetta Dellinger

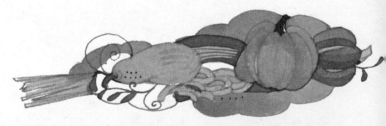

SPAGHETTI SQUASH

Purchase a spaghetti squash from a farmer's stand or from the supermarket. A spaghetti squash is a large golden squash. Show it to your class. Talk about it. Then cut off the stem and blossom ends. Either cover the squash with water and boil it whole until it is tender, or cut the squash in half and bake it upside down at 350° until tender (30-60 minutes).

When the squash is cool enough to handle, let students use a spoon to scoop out the insides. (As they scoop from top to bottom, the insides will come out in strings which look like spaghetti, but have fewer calories.)

Serve the squash as you would spaghetti, with a favorite spaghetti sauce.

JOHNNY CORNBREAD

Even the Pilgrims probably enjoyed delicious bread made from the new grain the Indians taught them to grow. Make some so your pupils can experience the mixing, smell, and taste.

1 c. yellow cornmeal
½ cup sugar
Pinch of salt
½ t. baking soda
1 t. cream of tartar

1 cup milk
1 well-beaten egg
1 T. honey
Pinch of ground ginger
1 T. melted butter

Preheat the oven to 375°. Sift the cornmeal, sugar, salt, soda, ginger, and cream of tartar together into a bowl.

Add all other ingredients, and stir together until well mixed.

Pour this mixture into a greased shallow baking pan or into castiron cornstick molds that you have heated in the oven and then greased. Fill the stick molds only ¾ full.

Bake 30 minutes.

by Dotti Hannum

SWEET PUMPKIN SQUARES

While the students are mixing and baking this recipe discuss:
Where did the Pilgrims get their spices?
Where did the Pilgrims get their pots and pans?
What did they use for pots and pans? How were theirs different from ours
today?

1 large pumpkin
1½ cups sugar
1 t. salt
2 t. ground cinnamon

1 t. ground ginger
½ t. ground cloves
2 cups evaporated milk or 3½ cups
half and half
4 eggs, slightly beaten

Day 1: Wash the pumpkin, and cut it into 8 pieces. Place the pumpkin sections, cut side down, in a pan. Bake it at 375° until the flesh is soft, but not mushy.

Scrape the flesh out of the pumpkin with a spoon or a fork. Place it in a colander, and let it drain overnight in a cool place.

Day 2: Put the pumpkin in a bowl, and whip it with a fork until all the lumps disappear. Drain out as much liquid as possible. The pumpkin should be dry.

Mix the pumpkin with sugar, salt, cinnamon, ginger, cloves, evaporated milk or half and half, and eggs.

Pour the mixture into a rectangular cake pan. Bake it at 425° for 15 minutes. Then lower the temperature to 350° and bake it for 45 minutes, or until knife inserted in the center comes out clean. Cool and serve.

by Dotti Hannum

MORE CRAFTS

ACCORDION BOOKLET

Students will enjoy making this accordion-like booklet, while at the same time they improve their association/communication skills.

For this activity, you'll need to provide an 8-by-36-inch piece of white shelf paper, marked off into twelve 3-inch sections, for each student. Show the students how to fold the paper to make an accordion booklet. At the top of each section, have students write a letter of the word Thanksgiving, beginning with T on the first section. Have the students make the letters in color. On the chalkboard list the following:

T — a fierce jungle animal;
H— the opposite of cold;
A — a kind of fruit;
N — a sleep for a short while;
K — something we fly in the sky;
S — the star that gives light and heat;
G — a bird that looks like a duck but is larger and has a longer neck;
I — frozen water;
V — a large covered truck;
I — a baby;
N— the opposite of far;
G — a model of the world.

Give older students colored markers to write the answers to

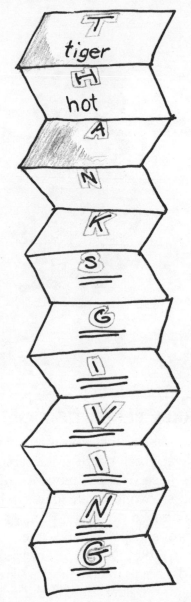

each phrase in the appropriate sections. Explain to the students that the answers they give must begin with the letters in the sections. (Answers: tiger, hot, apple or apricot, nap, kite, sun, goose, ice, van, infant, near, globe.)

TURKEY PENCIL HOLDERS

To make these turkey pencil holders, you'll need: small, empty, fruit juice cans; fabric scraps; scissors; white craft glue; white poster board.

Each student should trace and cut a turkey shape from poster board and from fabric. Have students glue the fabric to the poster board, and allow to dry. Place a piece of waxed paper and a weight of some kind (book, etc.) on top of the turkey to keep it flat while it's drying. Cover the juice can with the fabric. Glue the covered can to the turkey shape. Allow to dry.

Students will enjoy using their turkey pencil holders during the month of November as they anticipate the Thanksgiving holiday.

THANKSGIVING SEED
PICTURE

For each picture, you will need small seeds in light and dark colors, such as mustard and celery seeds; rug yarn; a small board or a piece of corrugated cardboard; a box top from a gift box; a glue-on picture hanger. Also provide pencils, rulers, scissors, a funnel or two, white craft glue, sandpaper, and clear acrylic spray (available at art supply stores).

Here are the steps:

1. Sand edges of boards, if rough.
2. Using a pencil, draw a Thanksgiving design on the board.
3. Put glue over all pencil lines. Glue rug yarn along the lines, cutting yarn as needed at the end of each line. Allow to dry.
4. Place the picture in the box top.
5. Cover inside of designs with glue.
6. Pour light colored seeds over the glue. Be generous with the seeds. Press seeds into the glue with your fingers.
7. Pour any excess seeds into the box top. Using a funnel, return unused seeds to the container. Allow picture to dry.

8. Place the picture in the box top.
9. Cover area outside of design with a coat of glue.
10. Sprinkle dark seeds over the glue.
11. Return excess seeds to container.
12. Allow picture to dry.
13. Spray picture with a clear acrylic finish. Allow to dry.
14. Attach a picture hanger. If you wish to make your own picture hanger, fold a short piece of yarn in half to form a loop. Tie a knot in each end of yarn. Tape loose yarn ends to back of picture.

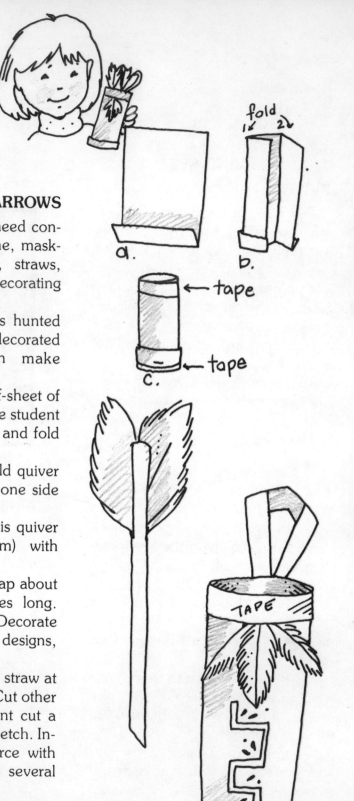

INDIAN QUIVER AND ARROWS

For materials you will need construction paper, cellophane, masking, or decorative tape, straws, feathers, scissors, and decorating supplies.

Talk about how Indians hunted and about ways they decorated their belongings. Then make quivers.

Give each student a half-sheet of construction paper. Tell the student to place paper lengthwise and fold up a 1-inch flap (see A).

With flap on outside, fold quiver into thirds (see B). Insert one side into the other (see C).

Let each student tape his quiver closed (sides and bottom) with decorative tape.

Have pupil cut paper strap about ½-inch wide and 6-inches long. Tape strap behind quiver. Decorate quiver with colorful Indian designs, feathers, and so forth.

To make an arrow, slit a straw at the top 1½-inches down. Cut other end to a point. Let student cut a feather out of paper as in sketch. Insert feather in slit. Reinforce with tape. Students may make several arrows each.

by Beth Holzbauer

POPCORN BOWLS

Have each child bring a good-sized plastic bowl to class. Provide foil, liquid laundry starch or your favorite papier-mâché medium, newspaper strips, tempera or acrylic paints, brushes, shellac, and protective coverings for the work area.

First have each student cover his bowl with aluminum foil. Then let each student dip paper strips in starch and use them to cover the outside of his bowl. The strips (papier-mâché) should be three or four layers thick. The children will need to let this dry a day or two.

When the bowls are dry, carefully remove the paper shells from the bowls. Also remove the foil.

Suggest that students paint their bowls a base color. Allow that to dry.

Each student may decorate his bowl with Indian signs and his name picture (page 32).

When the paint has dried, put a coat of shellac inside and outside of each bowl to make it more durable.

by Dotti Hannum

EGG CREATIONS

Before time to decorate the eggs, have the children blow the insides out of the eggs. To do this, put a small hole in each end of an egg. (You can do this with a hammer and small nail.) Then blow through one end to force the contents out the other. Blow the eggs into a bowl. Children enjoy doing this themselves. Try to use white eggs to make Pilgrims and brown eggs to make Indians and turkeys.

The materials you will need are eggs, paints or markers, empty cardboard tubes, black, white, yellow, and green construction paper, feathers, red (bumpy) chenille wire, cupcake baking cups, and glue.

Have each child choose which figure he would like to make. Caution the children that the eggs will break, if they are dropped or squeezed.

PILGRIM: Paint the face and hair for the Pilgrim on the egg. Let dry.

To make the Pilgrim's stand, cut a 1¼-inch deep section from a cardboard toilet-paper tube. Then cut a piece of black construction paper 5¼ by 1¼ inches. Also cut a white collar (see illustrations). Glue the black strip on the cardboard you cut. Then add collar.

To make the Pilgrim's hat, cut a black piece of construction paper 5¾ by ½ inches. Make this into a circular headband by stapling it

together so it fits around the egg. Cut a black hat and a yellow buckle. Glue them to the headband.

INDIAN: Paint face and hair of Indian on egg. Let dry.

Make the Indian's stand as described above. Draw an Indian design on a colorful piece of construction paper. Use it to cover the cardboard tube.

To make the Indian's headband, cut a piece of colorful construction paper 5¾ by ½ inches. Overlap the band about ½ inch (so it fits egg), and staple it in back. Staple a feather to the back of the band. (Use a real feather, or cut one out of construction paper.)

TURKEY: Glue paper turkey wings on the egg. Let dry.

To make a turkey stand, cut a green piece of construction paper as directed above to glue onto cardboard tube. Cut some turkey feet from yellow paper, and glue them to the stand.

To finish the turkey, use red chenille wire (or see pattern) for the head. Stick one end of the red wire through the hole in the egg; bend it to form neck, head, and wattle. Cut turkey eyes out of construction paper or felt. Glue them on the head. Fold a baking cup in half. Glue the cup to the back of the egg for tail feathers.

by Beth Holzbauer

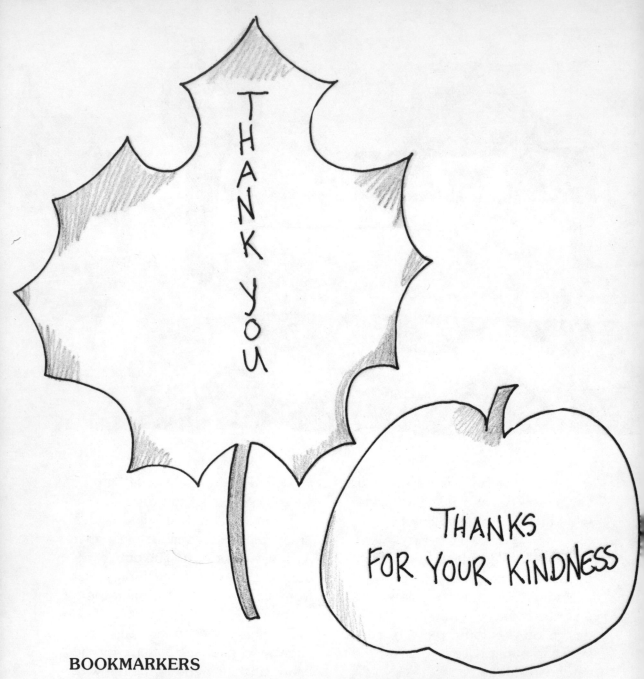

BOOKMARKERS

Students will enjoy making these leaf and pumpkin bookmarkers for themselves or to give as "thank-you" gifts on Thanksgiving Day.

To do this project, you'll need assorted felt scraps, white poster board, scissors, and white craft glue.

Trace and cut out the leaf and pumpkin patterns from the poster board. Make several patterns. Let the students use the patterns to cut leaves and pumpkins out of felt. Students may want to decorate their bookmarkers, using small felt scraps or alphabet letters.

SONGS
AND
POEMS

You Here Too

D.F.

Dorothy Farrow

No - vem-ber days are grow-ing short. It's time for sweat-ers and coats. And

Mom is bus - y fix - ing a great big tur - key roast. The

stuff-ing and the on-ions are wait-ing with a squash pie. And the

cran-ber-ry sauce in its spe-cial bowl looks beau-ti-ful to my eyes. Oh,

come a-long, come a-long Grand-pa. Bring Grand-ma o - ver too.

Come a-long o - ver to our house. We'll have Thanks-giv-ing for you. The

tur-key is in the o - ven. The ap - ple pie is made. Now

all we need is you here too, for a grand Thanks-giv - ing Day.

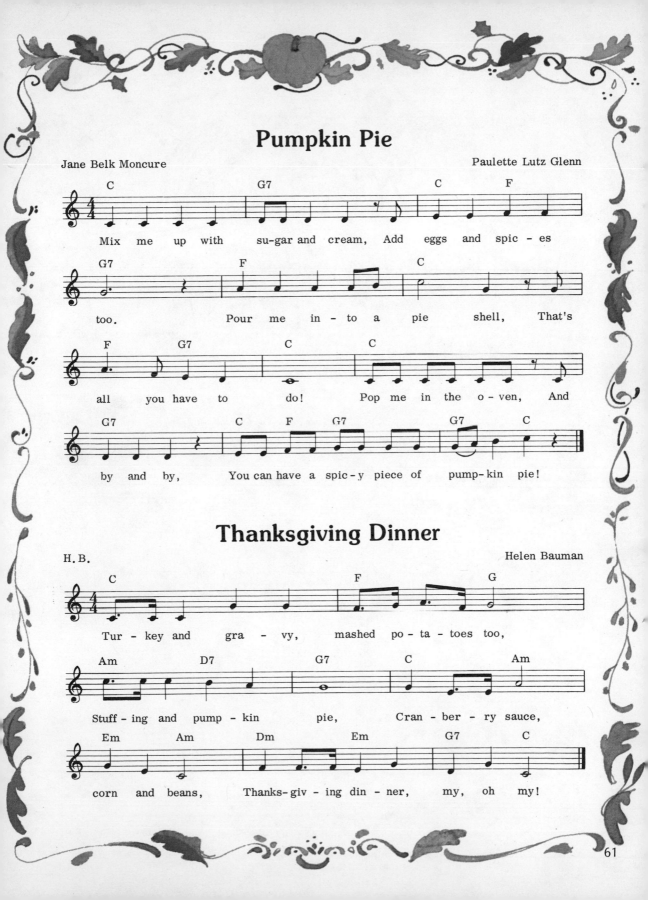

Pumpkin Pie

Jane Belk Moncure

Paulette Lutz Glenn

Mix me up with su-gar and cream, Add eggs and spic-es
too. Pour me in-to a pie shell, That's
all you have to do! Pop me in the o-ven, And
by and by, You can have a spic-y piece of pump-kin pie!

Thanksgiving Dinner

H.B.

Helen Bauman

Tur-key and gra-vy, mashed po-ta-toes too,
Stuff-ing and pump-kin pie, Cran-ber-ry sauce,
corn and beans, Thanks-giv-ing din-ner, my, oh my!

T is for Thanksgiving

Jane Belk Moncure

Jane Belk Moncure
Trans. by Paulette Lutz Glenn

T is for Thanks-giv-ing, H___ is for our homes so dear.

A is for the au-tumn, N for neigh-bors, far and near.

K is for the kitch-ens filled___ with spic-y pump-kin pies.

S is for the sun-shine in our hearts and in the skies. Oh, we'll

cel - e-brate Thanks- giv - ing Day and count our bless-ings too! And we'll

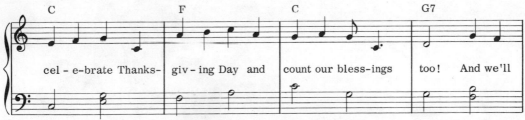

spell it T - H - A - N - K - S - giv-ing Day for you!

NOTE: Children would enjoy holding up signs which read T-H-A-N-K-S-GIVING Day as they sing the last four measures.

TOGETHER

Mother cooked the pumpkin.
Joan beat some eggs herself.
Father filled a cup with milk,
And brought some spices from the
    shelf.
John said he'd bring the sugar.
"I'll mix it up," said Cy.
They put it in the oven,
And out came pumpkin pie.
                    by Sandi Veranos

SKINNY BERT

A young skinny turkey named Bert,
Made a pig of himself on dessert.
    That's how he got fat.
    He was warned about that!
And now he's the dinner for Mert.
        by Kay Wilson

NUTTING

"Patience, take the basket.
  "Peter, take the pan.
"Hurry to the woods nearby.
  "Bring all the nuts you can."

Patience filled her basket.
  Peter filled his pan.
They fed some nuts to squirrels.
  Then home they quickly ran.

Mother said, "Oh, thank you,
  "So many nuts; that's dandy!"
She saved a sack but with the rest,
  She made them brown nut
  candy.

by Kay Wilson

THE VISITOR

A Pilgrim came to my house
  To spend Thanksgiving Day.
At first he seemed so frightened,
  I thought he'd run away.

I guess he heard the gunshots
  From the program on T.V.
And thought someone would get us
  If he stayed too long with me.

But then I took him with me
  To see the T.V. show.
And now that he is watching,
  He doesn't want to go.

by Sandi Veranos

TWO THANK YOUS

Charity Campbell sat on a log,
Making a doll by the cranberry bog.
Little White Feather just happened
    to see,
And wanted to know, "Will you
    make one for me?"
Said Charity Campbell, "I'll teach
    you for fun.
Then you will be able to make
    yourself one."
"Oh, thank you," said Little White
    Feather that day.
"My doll should wear beads so I'll
    string them this way."
Then Charity Campbell watched
    and learned how.
And she can string beads like an
    Indian now.
"Isn't it nice we can share as we
    do?"
Said Charity Campbell, "White
    Feather, thank you."

by Sandi Veranos

THANKSGIVING

Thanksgiving came to our town
    Not on the holiday,
But when the big tornado
    Stopped here, then blew away.
It didn't hit the schools
    Or tear the stores all down,
Or knock out all the telephones
    While things were blowing
    'round.

Then when the storm was over
    And the people were okay,
Each person helped his neighbor
    Clean up the mess that day.
I heard the people talking,
    So I know that it is true.
The words you heard the most
    that day
    Were "please" and "oh, thank
    you."

by Kay Wilson

66

A THANKSGIVING FESTIVAL

PILGRIM COSTUMES

Directions for making hats for Pilgrim men and women are on page 76. Girls should wear long-sleeved, long dresses with hats, collars, and aprons. Boys should wear pants or knickers, jackets, hats, knee socks, and white collars and cuffs. Boys could wear the knee socks over their pants and tie ribbons around them—for a knicker look. Use the directions here to explain the procedures to the children. Let them make their own collars, cuffs, and aprons.

(Note: For Indian Costumes see page 43.)

PILGRIM COLLARS: You will need scissors, white paper towels or tissue paper, and cellophane tape.

Fold two paper towels or a half-sheet of tissue together and then in half again. Cut at an angle toward the fold to make a neck opening (see illustrations).

Open the last fold. Cut up the center front to the neckline. Use tape to reinforce the shoulder folds. Slip the collar around the neck and pin it in place if you wish.

PILGRIM CUFFS: Cut cuffs from white crepe paper as in illustration. Fasten cuffs to each child's sleeves with safety pins.

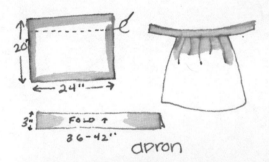

apron

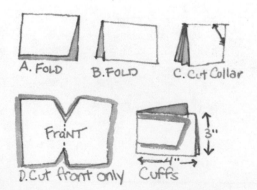

A. FOLD   B. FOLD   C. Cut Collar

FrONT

D. Cut front only   Cuffs   3"   4"

PILGRIM APRONS: Cut a rectangle of white crepe-paper. Use a large needle to put a drawstring along one edge. Cut a long strip, 4-inches wide, for the waistband. Fold in half. "Sew" it onto the gathered rectangle with staples, tape, or needle and thread.

DISPLAYS

If you use some of the learning activities suggested below, you will want to set up displays so that those who attend the festival may see what the children have done. The displays will also lend atmosphere to the festival.

HOMEMADE BUTTER: You will need one large jar with screw-on top, two cups of heavy cream or whipping cream, and ¼ t. salt.

Put the heavy cream and salt into the jar. Screw the top on tightly.

Let the children take turns shaking the jar. They may chant "Come, butter, come," or make up their own chants.

Keep shaking until the mixture "gathers" and looks like soft butter. Put the mixture in a small bowl or cup, and spread it on any bread. It's very good on Johnny Cornbread (page 49)!

Discuss: Does our butter look different from butter we buy in the store? How is it different? Does it taste different?

EASY SOAP: Pilgrims melted fat and lard. They mixed it with lye to make soap. Children often had to stir soap for hours, and they did *not* enjoy it! Soap is still made much the same way today. But it is done in factories. And other things such as glycerine, perfumes, and oils are often added to the soap.

To make soap the easy way, you will need: left-over pieces of soap, two cups of water, a double boiler, a hot plate or stove burner, ice cube trays, and a grater or sharp knife.

Let the children grate or cut up slivers of soap. Mix the soap with an equal amount of water, and let it soak overnight.

Put two cups of water in the bottom of a double boiler. Put the soap mixture in the top of double boiler. As it is melting over medium-high heat, let pupils take turns stirring the soap.

When the soap mixture is like a thick pudding, pour it into the ice cube trays. When the soap cubes are set, let the children pop them out. They may decorate the soap cubes with decals.

MAPLE SYRUP CANDY: In March the sap begins to run in the maple trees. The Indians showed the Pilgrims how to harvest the sap. First, they made holes in the trees and put in spouts. The sap ran through the spouts into buckets. When the buckets were filled, they poured the sap into big kettles. Children loved helping. Everyone had a sugaring-off party. The hot syrup bubbled away in the kettles. Everyone played games and sang and danced. They poured some of the syrup on clean snow and ate homemade maple candy. The rest of the sap boiled down into sugar.

To make similar candy you will need a large pot with a heavy bottom, long-handled wooden spoons, a cup filled with ice water, a large dishpan filled with clean snow or finely crushed ice, and 1½ cups of maple syrup.

Put the maple syrup into the pan. Boil the syrup without stirring until it reaches the hard-crack stage. (Drop a small bit of syrup into a cup of ice water. If the syrup separates into hard threads, it has reached the hard-crack stage.)

Slowly pour the hot syrup over the pan of clean packed snow or finely crushed ice. The candy cools quickly into "leather aprons" (strips).

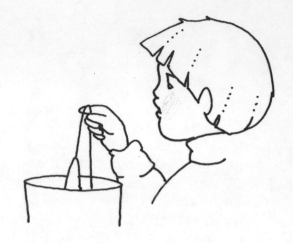

HAND-DIPPED CANDLES: The Pilgrims made their own candles. They dipped a length of wick over and over again into melted wax. Slowly the wax built into thicker layers with every dipping, and it formed a candle.

To make candles you will need one 18-inch length of wick for each student, a lead sinker, a double boiler, a hot plate or heat source, and paraffin wax.

Melt the paraffin wax in the double boiler over heat.

Give each child a length of wick with a weight on it. Let the children line up and take turns dipping their wicks, first in the wax, then in cold water. After the wick is dipped, the child will walk around to the back of the line. As each student reaches the pot again, his first layer of wax will be dry. He may want to roll the candle on a hard surface and shape it, then he can dip it again.

Keep dipping until each candle is

Really, all the Pilgrims were important. Each one had a job to do. The men explored the new land, took care of the women and children, hunted animals, and built homes. Women fixed the food, washed and patched clothes, sewed, helped the sick, made soap and candles, and took care of their children.

Young girls learned to sew aprons, knit stockings, and rock a baby's cradle. Older girls could weave cloth, pound corn into meal, and help make soap and candles. Boys helped their fathers by pulling weeds, guarding the garden, and gathering wood, nuts, and berries. Children had little time to play. But their favorite toys were rag dolls, balls, and whittled wooden toys. Children liked to go swimming, clamming, and fishing. There were no schools, but their parents found time to teach the children the alphabet and religion.

ACTIVITIES

1. I'M GOING TO SAIL ON THE MAYFLOWER. Before playing this game, talk about things the Pilgrims would have needed in a new land that had no stores: clothing, food, dishes, cooking pans, tools, weapons, goods to trade.

Ask the children to sit in a circle. Explain: the first child says, "I'm going to sail on the Mayflower and take my *hat*." The next child must repeat, "I'm going to sail on the Mayflower and take my *hat* and a *dish*." The next child must repeat the list and add what he is going to take. If a child forgets an item on the list, he leaves the circle. The last one in the circle is the winner.

2. PILGRIMS' MATH. Older children may answer by using number sentences.

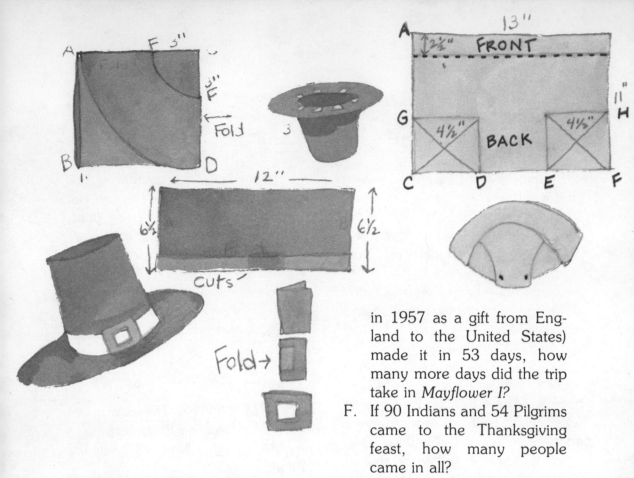

A. If Betsy had 5 kernels of corn to eat and Deborah had 5 kernels to eat also, how many did they have in all?

B. If Pilgrim men built 11 houses and there were 15 families, how many more houses did they need to build if each family were to have a house?

C. Jonathan caught 4 fish. Nathan caught 5 fish. Roger didn't catch any. How many did they catch altogether?

D. If Mary made 10 candles and her family burned 2, how many candles were left?

E. If *Mayflower I* crossed the Atlantic in 66 days and *Mayflower II* (which crossed the Atlantic in 1957 as a gift from England to the United States) made it in 53 days, how many more days did the trip take in *Mayflower I?*

F. If 90 Indians and 54 Pilgrims came to the Thanksgiving feast, how many people came in all?

3. PILGRIM HAT. Children enjoy dressing up as Pilgrims. Let them make hats.

To make the brim of a Pilgrim man's hat, cut a 14-inch square of black construction paper. Fold the square in half twice. Cut a curve from corner A to corner D and from E to F (both 3 inches from C). Open out flat to a doughnut shape.

To make the crown, cut a black strip 6½-by-12-inches long. Fold up 1 inch along the bottom. Cut 1-inch slashes at intervals on the flap. Fold up the tabs.

Overlap edges A & B ½ inch and staple. Glue the tabs to the underside of hat brim (sketch 3).

To make the buckle, cut a yellow construction paper rectangle 2 by 3 inches. Fold it in half lengthwise and cut out the center. Glue the buckle on the front of the hat.

PILGRIM CAP. To make a Pilgrim cap for a woman or girl, cut a rectangle 11 by 13 inches from white construction paper.

Along one edge, fold back 2½ inches.

Cut squares 4½ inches from corners C and F. Overlap corner G and D and staple. Overlap corner E and H and staple.

THE INDIANS OF PLYMOUTH
by Betty Foster

Indian pictures show up on cards, napkins, centerpieces, and other holiday decorations. Not only are pictures and likenesses of Indians used as symbols of Thanksgiving, but so are many things related to Indians—headdresses, peace pipes, corn, clothing, tepees, and so forth. That's because without their Indian friends, the Pilgrims might not have survived Three Indians—Samoset, Squanto, and Chief Massasoit— helped the Pilgrims the most. Samoset visited Plymouth first. He wanted to trade furs. The Pilgrims had brought brightly colored cloth, knives, beads, and small mirrors with them from England. They wanted to trade. They planned to send furs back to England to pay for the *Mayflower* and their supplies.

Samoset brought another Indian to Plymouth. He became the second important friend the Pilgrims made. His name was Squanto. He could speak English! He had once been captured and taken to Spain by traders. Squanto escaped to England. He learned English before he returned home. While Squanto was gone, his tribe, the Pawtuxet, was wiped out by sickness. The Pilgrims happened to settle where

Squanto's people had lived. That's why they had found cleared fields and buried baskets of corn at Plymouth. Squanto decided to stay with the Pilgrims. He could teach them how to live in this new land.

Squanto taught the Pilgrims which herbs and wild berries were safe to eat. The large fishhooks the Pilgrims had were too large to catch the fish nearby. Squanto showed them how to put fences made from willow branches across the small streams to catch the fish. Corn was new to the Pilgrims. Squanto showed them the Indian way to plant it. He said they must wait until the oak leaves were the size of mouse ears. Then they had to put two small herring-like fish (alewives) in each hole along with three or four seeds.

Squanto helped his white friends know what was happening in the Indian villages nearby. When the Pilgrims and Indians wanted to trade, Squanto helped them understand each other.

Massasoit was the Chief of the Wapanoags. He made a peace treaty with the Pilgrim leaders. The Indians and Pilgrims promised not to hurt each other. They did not rob each other or carry weapons when they visited each other. They sat on cushions on a green blanket and smoked the peace pipe. They agreed to be friends. The peace treaty lasted more than fifty years.

ACTIVITIES

1. AN INDIAN HEADBAND. Let each student cut a two-inch wide strip from the open end of a large grocery bag, and decorate it with Indian-like symbols. Try the band on the child. Make a fold in the strip to make it fit the child's head size. Remove the band; staple it to fit.

Let the child cut an 8-inch feather from a 3-by-9-inch rectangle of brightly colored construction paper. He can make 1-inch slashes in the edges so it will look like a feather.

Staple the feather at both the top and bottom of the headband.

Indian braves might wear Indian headbands, trousers with crepe-paper fringe sewn down the side seams, Indian vests, and long necklaces of wampum beads as their costumes for a festival.

2. MAKE CORNMEAL. Find a large flat rock with a shallow depression on top to hold some dried corn kernels. Clean the rock and place it on a soft towel spread out on the floor. Put a few kernels of dried corn on it.

Use a smaller smooth rock to pound the kernels until they are broken into fine particles of cornmeal. Make a display of the results.

3. POPCORN PICK UP. (The Indians taught the Pilgrims to love popcorn.) Provide a small bowl of popped popcorn for each child playing. Have each child empty his bowl into a pile on a napkin in front of him. At the signal to start, the child must use a large drinking straw to suck in, pick up a kernel, and move it to his empty bowl. The one who moves the most kernels in a pre-set time (three minutes) wins.

4. PLANT CORN. Soak three kernels of corn two or three hours in warm water. Obtain two or three dead fish from a pet store.

Fill a clay pot with potting soil. Make a two-inch deep hole in soil. Place the dead fish in the hole. Place the three kernels of corn on top of the fish. Cover with soil. Pat down soil and water it.

On a calendar mark off the days until the corn sprouts. Measure it once a week to see its growth. Later you may want to transplant the corn outside.

TURKEYS AND TRIMMINGS

by Betty Foster

What do you eat for Thanksgiving? Oven-roasted turkey with stuffing? Tasty cranberry sauce? Mashed potatoes and rich brown gravy? What kinds of vegetables do you choose? Squash? Peas? Broccoli? Green beans? Colorful salads made with cranberries? And what do you choose for desserts? Pumpkin pie? Mincemeat pie? Few of us grow the food that appears on our Thanksgiving table. We buy it at the store ready to cook. Our menu may be different from the Pilgrims' menu. We get our food in different ways. But the turkey and the trimmings are still important parts of nearly all American Thanksgiving celebrations. It's tradition!

Wild turkeys were plentiful in the New England forests in the 1600s. The settlers found they could capture the wild turkeys and raise them for food. Home grown birds were tastier and more tender. Years later only a few people raised their own Thanksgiving turkeys. Others bought theirs from a store. The price of turkeys was high. Most cooks only served turkey on Thanksgiving or Christmas. Today this has changed. With many farms raising thousands of turkeys, turkeys are cheaper. Now people are enjoying turkey more often.

No Thanksgiving feast would be complete without cranberries. The Indians taught the Pilgrims to eat

these tart, bright, red berries that grow on vines in the marshlands (bogs) of Cape Cod. Pilgrims thought the nodding pink blossoms on the vines looked like the heads of cranes. They called them *crane berries.* Or *cranberries* as we say it today. The Pilgrims ate the berries raw. They dried some for winter use. Sailors sometimes carried a supply of dried cranberries. They are high in vitamin C. Eating the berries helped to prevent scurvy.

ACTIVITIES

1. PINE CONE TURKEY PLACECARDS. Especially if you plan a party or feast, have the children make placecards as directed here. Put a pine cone on its side on a piece of clay or play dough. (Head will be at top of cone, tail at bottom.)

Glue a paper head and red wattle on the top of the cone. (It helps to have the heads, wattles, and feathers prepared in advance.)

Cut 3-by-½-inch strips from assorted bright colors of construction paper and shape them for tail feathers.

Glue the feathers on, one at a time, between the "petals" at the tail end of the cone.

Cut a 3-by-5-inch orange construction paper rectangle for each child. Have each child print his name at the bottom and set his turkey on the card.

2. HIDE THE TURKEY. To play this game you will need a turkey

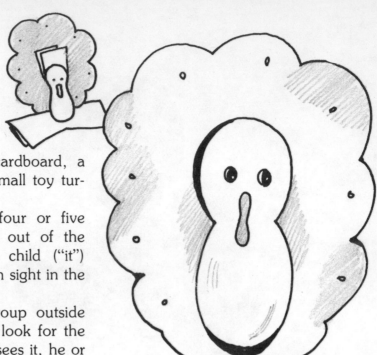

sticker backed with cardboard, a turkey cut-out, or a small toy turkey.

Send a group of four or five children at one time out of the room. Have another child ("it") hide the turkey in plain sight in the room.

At a signal, the group outside returns and begins to look for the turkey. When a child sees it, he or she goes quietly to his or her seat and *then* says, "Gobble! Gobble!" The rest of the children must search until they see it too. They do the same thing.

The one who spies the turkey first gets to hide it while another group goes out.

3. "LAND, FOREST, SEA— WHERE SHOULD IT BE?" In advance, print cards (or use pictures for younger children) for Thanksgiving food words such as: clam, cranberry, corn, turkey, fish, rabbit, etc. Place the cards in a box.

To play the game, each child draws a word and says it aloud. Then he says:

"Land, Forest, Sea.
Where should it be?"

The first student to answer correctly draws the next card and the game continues. You may divide

into teams and let players on each team take turns answering.

4. TURKEY NAPKIN HOLDER. For this project you will need a roll of colorful ribbon 2¾-inches wide, brown felt, red chenille wire, spring-type clothespins, moveable eyes, glue, and scissors.

Have each child cut a shell shape to use as feathers for his turkey from the ribbon (see pattern). Older students may also cut the head/body pieces out of felt (see pattern). To assemble their napkin holders pupils will glue the feathers onto clothespins (open parts at the bottoms). They will then glue the felt bodies on top of the feathers, add eyes and red wattles.

by Beth Holzbauer

THE HORN OF PLENTY

by Betty Foster

In America at Thanksgiving time, we often see a cornucopia or horn of plenty. The basket-like container looks like an oversized ice-cream cone lying on its side with its curved tip tilting up into the air. The cornucopia is filled to overflowing with fruits, vegetables, nuts, and/or flowers.

We borrowed the idea of the cornucopia as a symbol of plenty from the Greeks. The Greeks have a myth about Hercules, son of Zeus. He had a contest with the river god, Achelous. Achelous looked like a bull. Hercules jerked off one of his horns and won the battle. Then he filled the horn with flowers and gave it to Demeter, the goddess of plenty.

Still another myth says that when Zeus was a baby he was fed by the goat, Amalthea. Zeus took one of the goat's horns to give to his nurses for taking good care of him. The goat's horn was so special, it would fill itself up with whatever meat or drink its owner wanted.

Perhaps that is why the full animal horn became a symbol for plenty of food and a good harvest.

Today the cornucopia is often used on Thanksgiving cards. And you can find it on stickers.

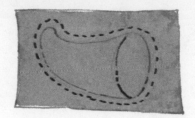

ACTIVITES

1. A CORNUCOPIA. Have the children make pictures of horns of plenty for their holiday decorations. Before class make a sample to display.

Have each pupil sketch and cut out a horn-shaped cornucopia from a 6-by-9-inch sheet of brown construction paper. (For younger children make the cornucopias in advance.)

Each pupil should glue his horn, a little left of center, onto a sheet of light blue construction paper (see sketch).

Have the children cut or tear freehand shapes of fruit and nuts from assorted colors of construction paper. They should paste the fruit, etc. at the open end of the horn. Remind them it is a horn of plenty. It sould seem to overflow!

2. STORY STARTER. (Younger children could do this in a supervised group, taking turns continuing the story orally. Let older students tell their own.)

Explain: pretend you have found *a magnificent magic horn of plenty.* It will give you any three wishes. What does the horn look like? What is the magic formula to make it work? What three things will you wish for? What will happen when you get your wishes? You may begin your story in your own way, or like this:

"Last Monday I was taking a walk in the woods. To my surprise, there beside the path I saw...." (You are to finish the story.)

3. WHAT WE ARE THANKFUL FOR. Place a large teacher-made cornucopia on a bulletin board. Fill it with outline pictures of fruit. As the children tell what they are thankful for, write the words on the pieces of fruit. Read the words back after you finish.

STORIES
TO READ
AND TELL

HATS

by Beth Holzbauer

It was a beautiful day to take a walk! The sky was a deep blue. Fast moving clouds seemed to say, "Come, follow me."

I walked down my street to my friend Mike's house. Nobody was home. I walked on.

By and by, I noticed a new little shop. HATS the big sign said. On the door a smaller sign said, "Come in. We're open." So I went in.

I knew at once this wasn't an ordinary hat shop. There were hats everywhere. Some were on shelves. Some were hanging from the ceiling. Some were in a glass case. And some were in boxes on the floor.

It was not the kind of place my mom would go to buy a hat. The hats were old—really old.

"That looks like Davy Crockett's hat," I said to myself. "And that looks like George Washington's hat."

"Ma'am," I said to the sales clerk, "may I try on these hats?"

"Yes, of course," she said.

I looked around the room. On the top shelf I saw a Pilgrim's hat. It was tall and black. I pointed to it. "I'd like that one, Ma'am."

She handed me the hat.

I climbed upon a stool. I put the hat on and looked in the mirror.

"Pretty good looking," I said. "I'd make a good Pilgrim."

Suddenly I found myself sitting at a long wooden table. More than a hundred Pilgrims and Indians were there. It was no ordinary picnic! Then I knew. I had gone from being a boy in a hat shop to being a Pilgrim at the first Thanksgiving feast.

Nobody seemed to see me. I

started to look around. So much food. Turkey, fish, clams, deer meat, and duck. I decided to taste them all.

Farther down the table were vegetables—corn, beans, squash, and pumpkins; and fruit—plums, grapes, cranberries. And nuts and corn cakes.

I tasted them all. Was I full! Actually, I could hardly move.

I started to listen. A man stood up and began to speak. He just had to be Governor Bradford.

"Remember our trip from England to America," Governor Bradford said. "For 66 days we sailed on the *Mayflower*. There was little food. Many of you were sick. The ship was crowded. But God brought us safely here to Plymouth, Massachusetts. Today we give thanks to God for His great love and care for us. God has given us

this food and good homes. We can thank God for the freedom we have found in this new land."

Another Pilgrim stood up. "I want to thank two special Indians, Samoset and Squanto, for all their help over the past year. They taught us how to plant corn, how to catch fish, and where to find good berries and nuts. They showed us how to dig for clams too. Without their help we would probably have starved to death."

"Starved to death?" I said to myself. "How could you starve to death here?" I looked around. There were no stores. And no restaurants either. They had to grow or find all their food by themselves.

An Indian stood up. Was he Squanto?

"We too remember when you first came to America. That winter

was cold. Half of your people died. But you didn't give up. You built houses for yourselves. And you worked hard. At first we were afraid of you. And you were afraid of us. Then we made a peace treaty. Now we are good friends. I am glad you came to America."

Everyone had finished eating. What will they do now? I wondered. The Indians sat together. The Pilgrims sat together. The Indians did a dance for the Pilgrims. Then they showed the Pilgrims how well they could shoot their bows and arrows.

The Pilgrims had a parade. The children played games. Such fun! Until somebody knocked off my hat.

Poof! I was back in the hat shop looking in the mirror. The Pilgrim's hat was on the floor. I picked it up, and laid it on the counter.

The sales clerk looked at her watch. "It's five o'clock," she said. "Time to close."

"Good-by, and thank you," I said. I ran down the street. I glanced back at the Hat Shop. Now the sign said, "Closed, come again."

"Thanks," I said. "I think I will."

Optional: Answer the following questions verbally or on paper.

1. What would you take with you on a trip from England to America?

2. What would you do while you were on the *Mayflower?*

3. What would you do when you first landed in America?

4. How would you build your new house?

5. What would you think of the Indians?

6. Would you rather fish or hunt for your food? Why?

7. How would you stay warm in the cold winter?

YELLOWHAMMER AND SITTING BULL

An Osage Indian Story

"I'm so sleepy," yawned a little Indian boy named Slow. Slow never was in a hurry. He always took his time. He stopped to think before he did something. An Osage Indian boy in the Dakota country could not be too careful.

Slow lay down under a cottonwood tree. He was soon fast asleep. Slow had walked a long way. He was hunting. And Slow had not caught even a rabbit or a squirrel.

In the branches over his head, a yellowhammer began to tap. *Rat-a-tat-tat! Rat-a-tat-tat!* Such a noise! Slow awoke with a start.

"Stop that noise! Can't you see I'm trying to sleep?" Slow asked the bird. But just then Slow heard another noise. He listened. Something was in the woods. Carefully, Slow looked around. He saw it. It was a great, brown grizzly bear.

"Ohh," breathed Slow. He was so frightened. What should he do? He couldn't run. "A bear runs faster than I do," he told himself.

"I could climb the tree. No! The bear could climb faster."

Slow stayed very still. His little arrows would never kill a grizzly bear. They would just make him mad.

"I'll play dead," Slow decided. And he did.

The great brown grizzly came right up to Slow. It sniffed his legs. It nosed around his moccasins. Slow could hear its huffing growls. Slow waited. He almost stopped breathing.

Suddenly the bear turned. It lumbered off into the woods. Still Slow did not move. For a long time the woods stayed still. Slowly Slow sat up.

"Yellowhammer," said Slow, "I thank you. You woke me up before the bear could surprise me. You saved my life. I will not forget. I will always be a friend to all Bird People because of you."

The little Indian boy that the yellow bird saved grew up to become an Indian chief. A great leader. He was not always called Slow. One day he got a new name—Chief Sitting Bull. And Chief Sitting Bull never forgot his promise to the yellow bird.

THE TURTLE'S SHELL

An Ojibway Indian Legend

(Indian children, like all children, love stories. Some Indian tribes had storytellers who passed along the fairy tales and wonder stories of Indian legend. A good storyteller could tell you how the robin got his red breast, how fire found its way into the forest, and even how the turtle got his shell. The story here is a re-telling of one such legend as an Indian child might have heard it.)

Long before the Indians roamed the lakes and forests of the far north, the mighty magician, Nanabush, hunted there. And he fished the waters.

"I have not even caught the tiniest fish," Nanabush said to himself one day. "And I have fished for hours on the great lake."

So Nanabush sat down to think. "Where shall I fish next?" he asked himself. As Nanabush sat thinking, he saw a turtle sunning itself.

Now back in the days when Nanabush roamed the forests, turtles did not have hard shells. In fact, their soft shells did not make much of a house for them at all.

And otters delighted to splash about playfully in the lake waters. Such an otter chanced to see the turtle taking a sun bath.

"Ahhh! That turtle shall be my dinner," said the otter. And he prepared to gobble up the turtle.

As it happened, the little turtle heard the otter coming. Quickly the turtle crawled under a piece of bark that had fallen from a nearby tree. He pulled his head and feet inside. The turtle was so well hidden that the otter could not tell where he was. In disgust, the otter slipped back into the water. Away he swam.

"How clever you are, Turtle," said Nanabush. "Since you're so smart, tell me where I'll find the fish."

"Certainly, Nanabush," said the turtle. He sent Nanabush to the deepest pool.

Nanabush set to work with his

fishing spear. Quickly he caught all the fish he could eat.

"I must thank Turtle," said Nanabush. He went back to find him.

"Thank you, Turtle. You have done me a favor. Now I shall do something for you."

Nanabush turned the piece of bark where the turtle had hidden into a hard shell. He placed another shell beneath it. Then Nanabush fastened the shell house around the turtle.

He had just finished when another otter decided on turtle for dinner.

"Don't be afraid," said Nanabush. "Stay right where you are.

See what happens. I will save you if need be."

Nanabush disappeared behind a tree. Otter sneaked up. He grabbed Turtle. Turtle pulled in his head and feet.

No matter how hard he tried, the poor otter could not get the turtle's shell open. Turtle was tucked safely inside. At last the angry otter gave up.

Nanabush laughed. He jumped from behind the tree.

"What a fine house you have now," he said. "All your children's children will wear shells too. People will see. They will know that you did Nanabush a favor. And Nanabush said thank you."

THE THANKSGIVING THE TURKEY GOBBLED

by Sandra Ziegler

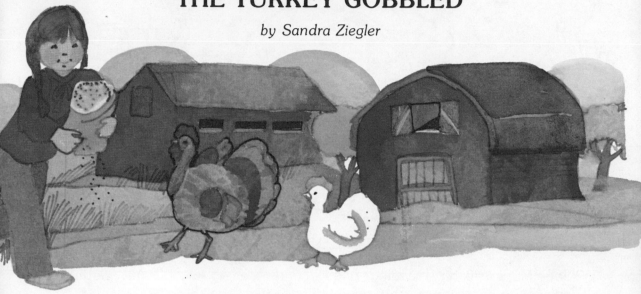

Sally Marie picked up her pan and scooped some poultry feed into it. She was not looking forward to stepping out into the autumn chill. But the barnyard critters needed their breakfast. Of course, she could be quick about scattering the feed. But Sally Marie knew she wouldn't. She never was. Most of the chickens had names, and she had to talk to each one.

Sally Marie was about to finish her morning chore when she heard a demanding gobble. "So you're hungry too, are you, Tom-Tom?" asked Sally. Her turkey had a name too. She had saved a special handful of feed for the big bird. And now Sally Marie threw some of it to him.

"I'm not sure I like you being so fat, Tom-Tom," said Sally Marie as she watched the turkey eating some corn. "Not with Thanksgiving next week. And not when Dad has lost the cows to sickness. Without money, we'll have to eat what we have this year. I hope that doesn't mean you."

Sally Marie knew that eventually all the birds on the farm would end up in the stew pot or oven. Mother had warned her about that. Still Sally Marie insisted on giving them names. And to her each bird was special.

"Your breakfast is ready," Mom called from the house.

"I've got to hurry, Tom-Tom, or I'll miss the school bus," Sally Marie told her turkey. She threw him a few more kernels of corn, closed the gate, and hurried back toward the house.

Her school was in town. And

Sally Marie was busy reading. She did not know that a call came in at the fire house. Oh, she heard the sirens. But Sally Marie did not know the truck raced along the same road that she had taken to school. She did not know that it stopped in her own farm yard.

"Save the barn! And the house! Hurry! Please, hurry!" Mother screamed as the firemen arrived.

The storage shed was already gone. And the flames were working away at the chicken coop as the firemen arrived.

Father looked on in disbelief. "First the cows, and now the chickens. And maybe even the house and barn," he said sadly. "I can't believe our luck is this bad."

The firemen went quickly to work. "It's under control," said the fire chief at last. "We will save the house and even the barn."

Father sighed. "Thank goodness for that," he said.

When she came up the road from school that afternoon, Sally Marie asked, "What happened? Where is the chicken house? Where are the birds?"

"Gone," said Father.

"We had a fire," said Mother. "The birds were frightened or trapped. And they are all gone."

"Even Tom-Tom?" asked Sally.

"Even Tom-Tom," said Mother.

"What will we do for Thanksgiving," asked Sally, "without any birds?"

Mother just shook her head.

The next morning Mrs. Bronson greeted Sally Marie as she walked into her class at school. "I heard you had a fire out at your place," she said.

"Yes," said Sally Marie. "All our poultry is gone."

"You lost your cows last summer too, didn't you?" asked Mrs. Bronson.

"Yes," said Sally Marie. "I don't know how we will have Thanksgiving this year. Even the turkey is gone."

"Can't you get a turkey at the supermarket?" asked Mrs. Bronson.

"They cost too much money," said Sally Marie. "We have to eat what we have on hand."

As Thanksgiving Day drew near, Mother did not mention it. Sally Marie did not like to ask about it. We probably just won't celebrate this year, she decided. And I guess they all decided the same thing.

For on the Barry farm that year, Mother did not make any pies. Father did not take down his axe and sharpen the blade. Nobody hung the Indian Corn. And on the dining room table no lace tablecoth appeared. There were no colorful arrangements of leaves and nuts, apples and gourds. And Sally Marie did not get her promised lesson on how to make corn-husk dolls.

Thanksgiving Day dawned a cool, sunshiny day. In the Barry kitchen no one hurried to light the oven and start the turkey cooking. There was no spicy smell of pump-

kin pies baking. And the sink was not piled with dishes dirtied in the preparation of the annual feast. Father went out to do some painting in the barn. Sally Marie could hear the hum of the sewing machine, and she knew Mother was busy upstairs. Sally Marie decided to read.

A demanding knock on the door brought Sally Marie swiftly back from the land of Oz. Sally Marie opened the door.

"It's time for dinner," said Mr. Kingsley. At his feet sat a large covered roaster. "Shall I take this straight to the kitchen?"

At first Sally Marie was speechless. "Mom!" she called at last. "Mom!"

Mother hurried down the stairs.

"Look," said Sally Marie, "everyone is here."

And they were. With pies and salads, sweet potatoes and corn, dressing and gravy, cornbread and jam. Such a feast has only been equaled by the Pilgrims that first Thanksgiving Day.

"What's all of this?" asked Father, coming in from the barn.

"We could not leave you to spend today alone," said the neighbors. "Bad luck could happen to any of us."

Mr. Kingsley offered to give Father some lumber and help him rebuild the chicken coop and the shed.

The Rices and the Browns promised to fill the silo, so there would be feed for the new cows they would be able to buy. Mr. Rice had worked out a plan with Mr. Gonzales at the bank, to see that Father would be able to get the money he needed.

And the farm women carried in box after box of home-canned food—peaches and pears, jelly and jam, corn and tomatoes. Soon the pantry shelves were filled.

"It truly is Thanksgiving after all," said Sally Marie, as everyone crowded into the dining room which was now bursting with food. "Oh, thank you all."

"Our neighbors are the dearest on earth," said Mother. She turned to open the window. With the crowd, it was suddenly warm inside.

"Yes," Father agreed. "We are so thankful for. . ." but he did not get to finish.

"Gobble, gobble," they heard.

At first everyone looked at the roasted turkey, sitting uncarved on the platter. It couldn't be.

"It's Tom-Tom," said Sally Marie. She raced to the window and looked out. "He's home."

"He sure timed that right," said Mother. And everyone laughed.

DATE DUE

	OCT 1 2 1989		
NOV 19 1989			